This journal belongs to:

Dear Reader,

Thanks for purchasing our book.

We feel grateful to serve you with our carefully created:
courage, Love & Happiness

& Hope you enjoy, learn and find what you're looking for.

All the best,

21 Exercises
& The True Potential Project Publishing Team

Imagination does not become great until human beings,
given the courage and the strength, use it to create.

Maria Montessori

courage, Love & Happiness

A Self-Discovery Journal For Women

Follow us on Instagram

For promotions, giveaways and newest arrivals

Instagram: 21exercises_journals

Courage, Love & Happiness

A Self-Discovery Journal For Women

Creative prompts

---

21 Exercises

The Start

Examine your potential.
Discover strength.

Creativity is the key to solutions.
The door that leads to answers.

Nurture it.

What would the world do without you?
So many souls that'd want to be touched...
So many persons waiting.

The world needs a fresh breeze of authenticity.
Of you, doing what you need to.
However small it may be.

The world needs you.
Your love.
Your talents.
Your everything.

Don't wait no longer,
The time is now.

It's up to you.

And now?

1. Turn the page, it's time to start.
2. There is now *how to*. Use this journal whatever way you want.
3. BUT... Try to be honest, brutally honest, as they say. Awareness is the first step towards development.
4. Honesty, creative efforts, and self-discovery: work the best when you give them your attention.
5. There is no right or wrong. It's all just a learning process.
6. Be kind to yourself, a journaling habit alone is worth a celebration.
7. Above all, drama enough, don't forget to be a smiling girl. What if we forget to enjoy life? To enjoy the process. It's gonna be a bumpy road for sure, but it's your, unique road. And that road, it's worth a smile. Every day.

At some point in life the world's beauty becomes enough.
You don't need to photograph, paint, or even remember it.
It is enough.

Toni Morrison

Date: ___ / ___ / _____

"What's meant to be
will always find a way"

Trisha Yearwood

Make a chronological timeline with the most significant incidents that define who you are today. You can use the next page as well.

"Love is too precious to be ashamed of."

Laurell K. Hamilton, *A Stroke of Midnight*

A conversation with your (ideal) lover, where you say the things you always wanted to say.

_____
_____
_____
_____
_____
_____
_____
_____
_____
_____
_____
_____
_____
_____
_____
_____
_____
_____
_____
_____
_____
_____
_____
_____
_____
_____
_____
_____

Date: ___ / ___ / _____

"In one aspect, yes, I believe in ghosts, but we create them. We haunt ourselves."

Laurie Halse Anderson, Wintergirls

A drawing, short story or poem expressing your critical self.

Date: ___ / ___ / _____

"If you judge people, you have no time to love them."

Mother Teresa

Seven small things you could do to improve your love life.

_____
_____
_____
_____
_____
_____
_____
_____
_____
_____
_____
_____
_____
_____
_____
_____
_____
_____
_____
_____
_____
_____
_____
_____
_____
_____
_____
_____
_____

Date: ___ / ___ / _____

"Your time is way too valuable to be wasting on people that can't accept who you are."

Turcois Ominek

What conventional thoughts about women, just don't work for you?

Date: ___ / ___ / _____

**"There is no greater agony
than bearing an untold story inside you."**

Maya Angelou, *I Know Why the Caged Bird Sings*

What the world would gain if you'd express yourself fully.

_____

_____

_____

_____

_____

_____

_____

_____

_____

_____

_____

_____

_____

_____

_____

_____

_____

_____

_____

_____

_____

_____

_____

_____

_____

_____

Date: ___ / ___ / _____

"We don't see things as they are, we see them as we are."

Anaïs Nin

The best 7-day diet that would work for you.

Date: ___ / ___ / _____

"There are two ways of spreading light: to be the candle or the mirror that receives it."

Edith Wharton

A drawing, short story or poem to express your sexual energy.

"Curiouser and curiouser!"

Lewis Carroll, Alice in Wonderland

A drawing, short story or poem
about a risk you should actually take.

"Sometimes it takes a good fall
to really know where you stand"

Hayley Williams

The last time you've been able to endure and raise
after a mistake or setback.

_____

_____
_____
_____
_____
_____
_____
_____
_____
_____
_____
_____
_____
_____
_____
_____
_____
_____
_____
_____
_____
_____
_____
_____
_____
_____
_____
_____
_____

Date: ___ / ___ / _____

"You don't love someone because they're perfect, you love them in spite of the fact that they're not."

Jodi Picoult

A list of all the people in your life you feel grateful for.

"Dress shabbily and they remember the dress; dress impeccably and they remember the woman."

Coco Chanel

What would be your favorite wardrobe?

_____
_____
_____
_____
_____
_____
_____
_____
_____
_____
_____
_____
_____
_____
_____
_____
_____
_____
_____
_____
_____
_____
_____
_____
_____
_____
_____

Date: ___ / ___ / _____

"Success means we go to sleep at night knowing that our talents and abilities were used in a way that served others."

Marianne Williamson

What's your definition of a successful woman.

_____
_____
_____
_____
_____
_____
_____
_____
_____
_____
_____
_____
_____
_____
_____
_____
_____
_____
_____
_____
_____
_____
_____
_____
_____
_____
_____
_____
_____

Date: ___ / ___ / _____

**"If I had a flower for every time I thought of you...
I could walk through my garden forever."**

Alfred Tennyson

Your love life, chronologically.
(You can use this page and the next.)

Date: ___ / ___ / _____

"A lady's imagination is very rapid; it jumps from admiration to love, from love to matrimony in a moment."

Jane Austen, *Pride and Prejudice*

How could you use your imagination to improve yourself?

_____
_____
_____
_____
_____
_____
_____
_____
_____
_____
_____
_____
_____
_____
_____
_____
_____
_____
_____
_____
_____
_____
_____
_____
_____
_____
_____
_____
_____
_____

"Curious that we spend more time congratulating people who have succeeded than encouraging people who have not."

Neil deGrasse Tyson

Imagine you were your own life coach, what are the three pieces of advice you would give yourself?

Date: ___ / ___ / _____

"Accepting oneself does not preclude
an attempt to become better."

Flannery O'Connor

What could you do to deal better with confrontation?

"There is no failure except in no longer trying."

Elbert Hubbard

Write down at least seven positive and encouraging affirmations you deserve.

"Sex is an emotion in motion."

Mae West

Your definition of a good sex life.
(And... Is it possible for you? If not, how could you make it possible?)

_____
_____
_____
_____
_____
_____
_____
_____
_____
_____
_____
_____
_____
_____
_____
_____
_____
_____
_____
_____
_____
_____
_____
_____
_____
_____
_____
_____

Date: ___ / ___ / _____

"Don't blow off another's candle for it won't make yours shine brighter."

Jaachynma N.E. Agu, *The Prince and the Pauper*

What makes you jealous of other women?
Try to be honest and list down all the reasons.
Awareness is the first step to change.

Date: ___ / ___ / _____

"Some things in life are out of your control.
You can make it a party or a tragedy."

Nora Roberts, *Vision in White*

A drawing, short story or poem to express your repressed anger.

"Don't aim for perfection.
Aim for 'better than yesterday."

Izey Victoria Odiase

When was the last time you were too hard on yourself?

"The real lover is the man who can thrill you by kissing your forehead or smiling into your eyes or just staring into space."

Marilyn Monroe

Draw or describe your perfect date night.

"Having something is not always better than not having it."

Beth Kempton, *Freedom Seeker*

Write down at least seven of your possessions you could easily live without.

Date: ___ / ___ / _____

"Have enough courage to trust love one more time and always one more time."

Maya Angelou

Describe your ideal love partner.

_____
_____
_____
_____
_____
_____
_____
_____
_____
_____
_____
_____
_____
_____
_____
_____
_____
_____
_____
_____
_____
_____
_____
_____
_____
_____
_____

"Don't be afraid of your fears. They're not there to scare you. They're there to let you know that something is worth it."

C. JoyBell C.

If the above quote is true, what are your fears trying to tell you?

Date: ___ / ___ / _____

"Doing the best at this moment puts you in the best place for the next moment."

Oprah Winfrey

Write down five things you could do
to integrate mindfulness into your daily life.

"Try to be a rainbow in someone's cloud."

Maya Angelou, *Letter to My Daughter*

A drawing, short story or poem expressing unique female qualities.

Date: ___ / ___ / _____

**"Drop the idea of becoming someone, because you are already a masterpiece. You cannot be improved.
You have only to come to it, to know it, to realize it."**

Osho

A drawing, poem or short story about being instead of trying.

**"Don't cry because it's over,
smile because it happened."**

Dr. Seuss

If you were the average of your five closest friends,
who would you be?

_____

_____

_____

_____

_____

_____

_____

_____

_____

_____

_____

_____

_____

_____

_____

_____

_____

_____

_____

_____

_____

_____

_____

_____

_____

Date: ___ / ___ / _____

"We accept the love
we think we deserve."

Stephen Chbosky, *The Perks of Being a Wallflower*

Write down your five biggest worries regarding your love life.
What would happen to these worries if you felt ten percent
more self-confident?

_____

_____

_____

_____

_____

_____

_____

_____

_____

_____

_____

_____

_____

_____

_____

_____

_____

_____

_____

_____

_____

_____

_____

_____

_____

_____

_____

_____

Date: ___ / ___ / _____

**"Often we look so long at the closed door
that we do not see the one which has been opened for us."**

Helen Keller

What five things are you most trying to control?

Date: ___ / ___ / _____

"There are years that ask questions and years that answer."

Zora Neale Hurston, *Their Eyes Were Watching God*

A bunch of questions today. Let's shine the spotlight on...
What is your worst habit?
Why do you feel the need to do it?
When do you most feel the need to do it?
Come up with three other habits you could integrate into your life
to replace the old habit.

Date: ___ / ___ / _____

**"Remain true to yourself, child. If you know your own heart,
you will always have one friend who does not lie."**

Marion Zimmer Bradley, *The Forest House*

A drawing, short story or poem representing your feelings about
having children (in the future, or not at all...).

Date: ___ / ___ / _____

"You yourself, as much as anybody in the entire universe, deserve your love and affection"

Sharon Salzberg

Write down all the reasons why you love yourself.
Come up with at least ten.

_____

_____

_____

_____

_____

_____

_____

_____

_____

_____

_____

_____

_____

_____

_____

_____

_____

_____

_____

_____

_____

_____

_____

_____

_____

_____

_____

_____

Date: ___ / ___ / _____

"Understanding is the first step to acceptance, and only with acceptance can there be recovery."

J.K. Rowling, *Harry Potter and the Goblet of Fire*

What are the top three things
you would like to understand about yourself, and why?

_____

_____

_____

_____

_____

_____

_____

_____

_____

_____

_____

_____

_____

_____

_____

_____

_____

_____

_____

_____

_____

_____

_____

_____

_____

_____

_____

Date: ___ / ___ / _____

"I have learned that as long as I hold fast to my beliefs and values – and follow my own moral compass – then the only expectations I need to live up to are my own."

Michelle Obama

Describe your moral compass.

_____
_____
_____
_____
_____
_____
_____
_____
_____
_____
_____
_____
_____
_____
_____
_____
_____
_____
_____
_____
_____
_____
_____
_____
_____
_____
_____

Date: ___ / ___ / _____

"If you ever find yourself in the wrong story, leave."

Mo Willems, *Goldilocks and the Three Dinosaurs*

A dialogue between you and your ex-lover, today.

Date: ___ / ___ / _____

"You have power over your mind - not outside events. Realize this, and you will find strength."

Marcus Aurelius, *Meditations*

Write down all the things you worry about, that are outside of your control. Then rip this page out of the journal.

When you're ready, burn the paper.

"We can live without religion and meditation, but we cannot survive without human affection."

Dalai Lama

Make a drawing, or write a short story/poem
to express your love to the world.

**"Fear is inevitable, I have to accept that,
but I cannot allow it to paralyze me."**

Isabel Allende, *The Sum of Our Days*

Make a chronological timeline with the most significant moments
where fear stopped you from doing what you had to do.

Date: ___ / ___ / _____

"Whenever I feel the need to exercise,
I lie down until it goes away."

Paul Terry

Make a whole list of joyful things you could do the next time you feel bored, lonely or down.

_____

_____

_____

_____

_____

_____

_____

_____

_____

_____

_____

_____

_____

_____

_____

_____

_____

_____

_____

_____

_____

_____

_____

_____

_____

_____

_____

Date: ___ / ___ / _____

"Look within -
there is no end!"

Malebo Sephodi

What lies are you frequently tell to protect your own image?

_____

_____

_____

_____

_____

_____

_____

_____

_____

_____

_____

_____

_____

_____

_____

_____

_____

_____

_____

_____

_____

_____

_____

_____

_____

_____

_____

_____

_____

_____

_____

"She refused to be bored chiefly because she wasn't boring."

Zelda Fitzgerald, *The Collected Writings*

A drawing, short story or poem portraying you as your most confident, courageous, kind and sexy self.

Date: ___ / ___ / _____

"Life is what happens to us
while we are making other plans."

Allen Saunders

A conversation with someone close to you, where your emotions get
triggered in a negative way.

_____
_____
_____
_____
_____
_____
_____
_____
_____
_____
_____
_____
_____
_____
_____
_____
_____
_____
_____
_____
_____
_____
_____
_____
_____
_____
_____

Date: ___ / ___ / _____

"Love is a fruit in season at all times and within reach of every hand."

Mother Teresa

The 5 people you are seeking approval from the most.

"Nothing in life is to be feared, it is only to be understood. Now is the time to understand more, so that we may fear less."

Marie Curie

Three inventive solutions to deal with social anxiety.

Date: ___ / ___ / _____

"No persons are more frequently wrong, than those who will not admit they are wrong."

François de La Rochefoucauld

A drawing, short story or poem celebrating the last time you were wrong! (And thus, learned something new:)...

Date: ___ / ___ / _____

"Beware, O wanderer,
the road is walking too."

Jim Harrison, *After Ikkyu & Other Poems*

What is your favorite way to learn a new skill?

Date: ___ / ___ / _____

"The truth is what I make it.
I could set this world on fire and call it rain."

Victoria Aveyard

Make a drawing or write a short story/poem
about your favorite delusions.

**"Push yourself. Don't Settle.
Just live well. Just LIVE."**

Jojo Moyes

What you would do with ten million dollars.

_____

_____

_____

_____

_____

_____

_____

_____

_____

_____

_____

_____

_____

_____

_____

_____

_____

_____

_____

_____

_____

_____

_____

_____

_____

_____

_____

_____

_____

_____

"Flirting is a woman's trade, one must keep in practice."

Charlotte Brontë, *Jane Eyre*

How your sex life would look like,
if you'd feel totally confident about your body.

_____

_____

_____

_____

_____

_____

_____

_____

_____

_____

_____

_____

_____

_____

_____

_____

_____

_____

_____

_____

_____

_____

_____

_____

_____

_____

_____

"Adventure is worthwhile in itself."

Amelia Earhart

Make a drawing or write a short story/poem
about you at a party full of strangers.

Date: ___ / ___ / _____

"The best way out is always through."

Robert Frost

Describe your biggest worry, with all the dramatic details. For one day you can drown yourself in self-pity.
Tomorrow, we take a different approach.

Date: ___ / ___ / _____

"Life is a drama full of tragedy and comedy.
You should learn to enjoy the comic episodes a little more."

Jeannette Walls, *The Glass Castle*

Today, pick the same worry as yesterday and write about it as if it was a comedy. Try to be funny and enjoy the exercise.

"You can be a thousand different women. It's your choice which one you want to be. It's about freedom and sovereignty. You celebrate who you are. You say, 'This is my kingdom.'"

Salma Hayek

If you had all the time in the world, what would you do first?

Date: ___ / ___ / _____

"Fill your paper
with the breathings of your heart."

William Wordsworth

A drawing, short story or poem
representing the story you need to tell this world.

Date: ___ / ___ / _____

"I like work: it fascinates me.
I can sit and look at it for hours."

Jerome K. Jerome

What you say to yourself when you're procrastinating.

Date: ___ / ___ / _____

"Happy girls
are the prettiest"

Audrey Hepburn

A perfect day of relaxation.

_____
_____
_____
_____
_____
_____
_____
_____
_____
_____
_____
_____
_____
_____
_____
_____
_____
_____
_____
_____
_____
_____
_____
_____
_____
_____
_____

Date: ___ / ___ / _____

"Feminism is the radical notion that women are human beings."

Cheris Kramarae

Your thoughts on feminism.

_____
_____
_____
_____
_____
_____
_____
_____
_____
_____
_____
_____
_____
_____
_____
_____
_____
_____
_____
_____
_____
_____
_____
_____
_____
_____
_____
_____

Date: ___ / ___ / _____

"We have the marvelous gift
of making everything insignificant."

Nikolai Gogol

How you are trying to seek security in life.

_____
_____
_____
_____
_____
_____
_____
_____
_____
_____
_____
_____
_____
_____
_____
_____
_____
_____
_____
_____
_____
_____
_____
_____
_____
_____
_____
_____
_____

Date: ___ / ___ / _____

"Burdens are for shoulders strong enough to carry them."

Margaret Mitchell, Gone with the Wind

A drawing, short story or poem
representing your relationship with your parents.

Date: ___ / ___ / _____

"We all live with the objective of being happy; our lives are all different and yet the same."

Anne Frank

How you think the world sees you.

_____
_____
_____
_____
_____
_____
_____
_____
_____
_____
_____
_____
_____
_____
_____
_____
_____
_____
_____
_____
_____
_____
_____
_____
_____
_____
_____
_____
_____
_____

"Happiness always looks small while you hold it in your hands, but let it go, and you learn at once how big and precious it is."

Maxim Gorky

Three pieces of advice from your 70-year old self.

Date: ___ / ___ / _____

"Even when you have doubts, take that step. Take chances. Mistakes are never a failure—they can be turned into wisdom."

Cat Cora

Make a drawing or write a short story/poem
about your early childhood.

"I'm not in this world to live up to your expectations and you're not in this world to live up to mine."

Bruce Lee

Make a drawing or write a short story/poem
about your teenage years.

Date: ___ / ___ / _____

**"It was love at first sight, at last sight,
at ever and ever sight."**

Vladimir Nabokov, *Lolita*

Make a drawing or write a short story/poem
about the first time you fell in love.

"Blessed are the hearts that can bend; they shall never be broken."

Albert Camus

What social media and advertising do to your self-image.

Date: ___ / ___ / _____

"When I'm good, I'm very good, but when I'm bad, I'm better. "

Mae West

Make a drawing or write a short story/poem about the beautiful imperfections of your body.

Date: ___ / ___ / _____

"A smile is a curve
that sets everything straight."

Phyllis Diller

Your favorite roadmap for procrastination.

Date: ___ / ___ / _____

**"Always be a first-rate version of yourself
and not a second rate version of someone else."**

Judy Garland

The road towards self-acceptance.

Date: ___ / ___ / _____

"We are always the same age inside."

Gertrude Stein

The road towards self-confidence.

Date: ___ / ___ / _____

"Be the living expression of God's kindness: kindness in your face, kindness in your eyes, kindness in your smile."

Mother Teresa

The road towards mindfulness.

"The question is not what you look at, but what you see."

Henry David Thoreau

What if you were wrong about everything?

Date: ___ / ___ / _____

"Learn the rules, break the rules, make up new rules, break the new rules."

Marvin Bell

What social conditions just don't work for you?

_____
_____
_____
_____
_____
_____
_____
_____
_____
_____
_____
_____
_____
_____
_____
_____
_____
_____
_____
_____
_____
_____
_____
_____
_____
_____
_____
_____
_____

**"Freeing yourself was one thing,
claiming ownership of that freed self was another."**

Toni Morrison, *Beloved*

Your definition of freedom.
(And how you would cope with it...)

Date: ___ / ___ / _____

"Luxury is not a necessity to me, but beautiful and good things are."

Anais Nin

What material possessions just make you feel happy?

_____
_____
_____
_____
_____
_____
_____
_____
_____
_____
_____
_____
_____
_____
_____
_____
_____
_____
_____
_____
_____
_____
_____
_____
_____

"Now that she had nothing to lose, she was free."

Paulo Coelho, *Eleven Minutes*

What do you have to lose?
(That makes you feel stuck.)

Date: ___ / ___ / _____

"The earth laughs in flowers."

Ralph Waldo Emerson

The one mistake you keep repeating when it comes to enjoying life.

_____
_____
_____
_____
_____
_____
_____
_____
_____
_____
_____
_____
_____
_____
_____
_____
_____
_____
_____
_____
_____
_____
_____
_____
_____
_____
_____
_____
_____
_____

Date: ___ / ___ / _____

"Self-respect. It would make me lovable.
And it's the secret to good sex."

Susan Sontag, *As Consciousness is Harnessed to Flesh*

What does your sex life say about you as a person?

"You have everything needed for the extravagant journey that is your life."

Carlos Castaneda

Everything you've got inside you to make the extravagant journey.

_____

_____

_____

_____

_____

_____

_____

_____

_____

_____

_____

_____

_____

_____

_____

_____

_____

_____

_____

_____

_____

_____

_____

_____

_____

_____

_____

_____

_____

Date: ___ / ___ / _____

"Good sex is like good bridge. If you don't have a good partner, you'd better have a good hand."

Mae West

Your demands for a good sex partner.

"Men go to far greater lengths to avoid what they fear than to obtain what they desire."

Dan Brown, *The Da Vinci Code*

Your favorite roadmap for avoiding change.

Date: ___ / ___ / _____

**"The more clearly we can focus our attention on the wonders
and realities of the universe about us,
the less taste we shall have for destruction."**

Rachel Carson

A chronological timeline describing your working life.

Date: ___ / ___ / _____

"To survive, you must tell stories."

Umberto Eco, *The Island of the Day Before*

Make a drawing, or write a story/poem
about a past achievement that makes you feel proud.

Date: ___ / ___ / _____

"I think there should be a rule that everyone in the world should get a standing ovation at least once in their lives."

R.J. Palacio, *Wonder*

Make a drawing, or write a story/poem
about what gives you hope.

Date: ___ / ___ / _____

"One must dare to be happy. "

Gertrude Stein

Make a drawing, or write a story/poem
about being a woman in this world.

Date: ___ / ___ / _____

"Many people will walk in and out of your life, but only true friends will leave footprints in your heart"

Eleanor Roosevelt

Why you're grateful for your closest friends.

_____
_____
_____
_____
_____
_____
_____
_____
_____
_____
_____
_____
_____
_____
_____
_____
_____
_____
_____
_____
_____
_____
_____
_____
_____
_____
_____
_____

Date: ___ / ___ / _____

"Maybe some people
are just meant to be in the same story."

Jandy Nelson, I'll Give You the Sun

What do you have to offer in a romantic relationship?

_____
_____
_____
_____
_____
_____
_____
_____
_____
_____
_____
_____
_____
_____
_____
_____
_____
_____
_____
_____
_____
_____
_____
_____
_____
_____
_____

Date: ___ / ___ / _____

"You alone are enough.
You have nothing to prove to anybody."

Maya Angelou

When was the last time you felt the need
to prove yourself to someone?

Date: ___ / ___ / _____

"Happiness is something that comes into our lives through doors we don't even remember leaving open."

Rose Wilder Lane

Your definition of happiness.

_____
_____
_____
_____
_____
_____
_____
_____
_____
_____
_____
_____
_____
_____
_____
_____
_____
_____
_____
_____
_____
_____
_____
_____
_____
_____
_____
_____

"You're something between a dream and a miracle."

Elizabeth Barrett Browning

What other people could learn from you.

Date: ___ / ___ / _____

"The impossible could not have happened, therefore the impossible must be possible in spite of appearances."

Agatha Christie, *Murder on the Orient Express*

When was the last time you did something impossible?

_____
_____
_____
_____
_____
_____
_____
_____
_____
_____
_____
_____
_____
_____
_____
_____
_____
_____
_____
_____
_____
_____
_____
_____
_____
_____
_____
_____
_____
_____

Date: ___ / ___ / _____

"If you let people into your life a little bit, they can be pretty damn amazing."

Sherman Alexie, *The Absolutely True Diary of a Part-Time Indian*

What does it take to gain your trust?

Date: ___ / ___ / _____

"There is a crack in everything.
That's how the light gets in."

Leonard Cohen

Make a drawing or write a short story/poem
about your insecurities.

"The finest of pleasures are always the unexpected ones."

Erin Morgenstern, *The Night Circus*

Make a drawing or write a short story/poem about the last time something out of the blue guided you the right way.

"The real voyage of discovery consists not in seeking new landscapes, but in having new eyes."

Marcel Proust

A chronological timeline of your self-development over the years.

"Don't let the bastards grind you down."

Margaret Atwood, *The Handmaid's Tale*

How could you let your strengths blossom fully?

Date: ___ / ___ / _____

"Sometimes love means letting go when you want to hold on tighter."

Melissa Marr, *Ink Exchange*

What mistake do you make repeatedly
when it comes to your love life?

_____

_____

_____

_____

_____

_____

_____

_____

_____

_____

_____

_____

_____

_____

_____

_____

_____

_____

_____

_____

_____

_____

_____

_____

Date: ___ / ___ / _____

"Trees that are slow to grow
bear the best fruit."

Moliere

What do you need in your life right now: patience or action? Why?

_____

_____

_____

_____

_____

_____

_____

_____

_____

_____

_____

_____

_____

_____

_____

_____

_____

_____

_____

_____

_____

_____

_____

_____

_____

Date: ___ / ___ / _____

"To put everything in balance is good, to put everything in harmony is better."

Victor Hugo

Three questions you would ask one of your role models.

_____
_____
_____
_____
_____
_____
_____
_____
_____
_____
_____
_____
_____
_____
_____
_____
_____
_____
_____
_____
_____
_____
_____
_____
_____
_____
_____

"You live but once;
you might as well be amusing."

Coco Chanel

For the coming week make the commitment to treat yourself in a way that feels good for you, for at least three days. Write down what and when you're going to do it.

Date: ___ / ___ / _____

"When will you learn
that there isn't a word for everything?"

Nicole Krauss, *The History of Love*

A conversation with yourself as a teenager.

_____
_____
_____
_____
_____
_____
_____
_____
_____
_____
_____
_____
_____
_____
_____
_____
_____
_____
_____
_____
_____
_____
_____
_____
_____
_____
_____
_____

"No winter lasts forever;
no spring skips its turn."

Hal Borland

What could other people learn from you
when it comes to self-acceptance?

Date: ___ / ___ / _____

"We do not need magic to transform our world.
We carry all of the power we need inside ourselves already."

J.K. Rowling

The strengths and qualities that make you more than worthwhile
and important in this world.

_____
_____
_____
_____
_____
_____
_____
_____
_____
_____
_____
_____
_____
_____
_____
_____
_____
_____
_____
_____
_____
_____
_____
_____
_____
_____

**"Sometimes things fall apart
so that better things can fall together"**

Marilyn Monroe

When are you taking yourself too seriously?

Date: ___ / ___ / _____

"Where words leave off, music begins."

Heinrich Heine

How could you use your creativity to achieve your goals?

_____
_____
_____
_____
_____
_____
_____
_____
_____
_____
_____
_____
_____
_____
_____
_____
_____
_____
_____
_____
_____
_____
_____
_____
_____
_____
_____

"There is never a time or place for true love. It happens accidentally, in a heartbeat, in a single flashing, throbbing moment."

Sarah Dessen, *The Truth About Forever*

Describe in detail your most gorgeous, self-confident appearance on a night out.

Date: ___ / ___ / _____

"My philosophy is that worrying means you suffer twice."

J.K. Rowling, *Fantastic Beasts and Where to Find Them*

What conventional thoughts about women,
are actually totally working for you?

_____

_____

_____

_____

_____

_____

_____

_____

_____

_____

_____

_____

_____

_____

_____

_____

_____

_____

_____

_____

_____

_____

_____

_____

_____

_____

_____

_____

"Never underestimate the infinite love within you. It has the power to transform lives"

Mimi Novic, *The Silence Between the Sighs*

A letter to your (future) lover.

Date: ___ / ___ / _____

"If you never dream to be,
you'll never become."

Jenna Alatari

A remarkable dream you still remember and what it could mean.

_____

_____

_____

_____

_____

_____

_____

_____

_____

_____

_____

_____

_____

_____

_____

_____

_____

_____

_____

_____

_____

_____

_____

_____

_____

_____

_____

_____

_____

_____

_____

Date: ___ / ___ / _____

"No woman gets an orgasm
from shining the kitchen floor. "

Betty Friedan

Your three favorite sexual fantasies.

_____
_____
_____
_____
_____
_____
_____
_____
_____
_____
_____
_____
_____
_____
_____
_____
_____
_____
_____
_____
_____
_____
_____
_____
_____
_____
_____
_____
_____
_____

**"Do not spoil what you have by desiring what you have not;
remember that what you now have
was once among the things you only hoped for."**

Epicurus

Look in the mirror for at least one minute straight.
Describe what you see and feel.

_____
_____
_____
_____
_____
_____
_____
_____
_____
_____
_____
_____
_____
_____
_____
_____
_____
_____
_____
_____
_____
_____
_____
_____
_____
_____
_____

Date: ___ / ___ / _____

**"All my days I have longed equally to travel the right road
and to take my own errant path."**

Sigrid Undset, *Kristin Lavransdatter*

How are you most frequently misunderstood by other people?

Date: ___ / ___ / _____

"People do not change,
they are merely revealed."

Anne Enright, The Gathering

What is hidden under the surface?

_____
_____
_____
_____
_____
_____
_____
_____
_____
_____
_____
_____
_____
_____
_____
_____
_____
_____
_____
_____
_____
_____
_____
_____
_____
_____

"If you concentrate on what you don't have, you will never, ever have enough."

Oprah Winfrey

Make a drawing or write a short story/poem about you when you're loaded with anxiety.

**"With enough courage,
you can do without a reputation."**

Margaret Mitchell

Draw a graph representing your life over the last 12 months.

"All happiness depends on courage and work."

Honoré de Balzac

Draw a graph representing your finances over the last 3 years.

**"I must be a mermaid, Rango.
I have no fear of depths and a great fear of shallow living."**

Anais Nin

Make a timeline of how you would want your life turn out to be over the next 10 years.

"You may be the only person left who believes in you, but it's enough. It takes just one star to pierce a universe of darkness."

Richelle E. Goodrich, *Smile Anyway*

Who and what makes you feel optimistic about yourself and about life in general?

_____
_____
_____
_____
_____
_____
_____
_____
_____
_____
_____
_____
_____
_____
_____
_____
_____
_____
_____
_____
_____
_____
_____
_____
_____
_____

Date: ___ / ___ / _____

"The past is never where you think you left it."

Katherine Anne Porter

A drawing, short story or poem
to express your regrets about the past.

Date: ___ / ___ / _____

"I am beginning to learn that it is the sweet, simple things of life which are the real ones after all."

Laura Ingalls Wilder

Draw a timeline representing your appearance over the last 10 years.
(Tip: use old photos:)!

Date: ___ / ___ / _____

"Be glad. Be good. Be brave."

Eleanor Hodgman Porter

A drawing, short story or poem to express your courage.

"Life is a mirror: if you frown at it, it frowns back; if you smile, it returns the greeting."

William Makepeace Thackeray

A drawing, short story or poem to express joy for life.

Date: ___ / ___ / _____

"It is better to be hated for what you are than to be loved for what you are not."

Andre Gide, *Autumn Leaves*

Seven things that make you proud of your past.

_____
_____
_____
_____
_____
_____
_____
_____
_____
_____
_____
_____
_____
_____
_____
_____
_____
_____
_____
_____
_____
_____
_____
_____
_____
_____

**"At the end of the day,
we can endure much more than we think we can."**

Frida Kahlo

A drawing, short story or poem to express your perseverance.

"The best way to cheer yourself is to cheer somebody else up."

Albert Einstein

A drawing, short story or poem to express your optimism.

**"We are addicted to our thoughts.
We cannot change anything if we cannot change our thinking."**

Santosh Kalwar, Quote Me Everyday

A drawing, short story or poem about your ever rushing thoughts.

"The creation of a thousand forests is in one acorn."

Ralph Waldo Emerson

What small habits or tiny deeds are having a major influence on your overall well-being? Try to explain why.

_____
_____
_____
_____
_____
_____
_____
_____
_____
_____
_____
_____
_____
_____
_____
_____
_____
_____
_____
_____
_____
_____
_____
_____
_____

Date: ___ / ___ / _____

"Don't spend time beating on a wall, hoping to transform it into a door."

Coco Chanel

Your ideal workweek.

_____
_____
_____
_____
_____
_____
_____
_____
_____
_____
_____
_____
_____
_____
_____
_____
_____
_____
_____
_____
_____
_____
_____
_____
_____
_____
_____
_____
_____

Date: ___ / ___ / _____

"The earth has its music
for those who will listen."

Reginald Vincent Holmes, *Fireside Fancies*

A drawing, short story or poem
about what you'd love to do when you were young.

"I like good strong words that mean something..."

Louisa May Alcott, *Little Women*

A drawing, short story or poem
about the last time you surprised yourself.

Date: ___ / ___ / _____

"There are no ordinary moments."

Dan Millman, *Way of the Peaceful Warrior*

What problems in your life could actually be opportunities?

_____

_____

_____

_____

_____

_____

_____

_____

_____

_____

_____

_____

_____

_____

_____

_____

_____

_____

_____

_____

_____

_____

_____

_____

_____

"People change and forget to tell each other."

Lillian Hellman

A drawing, short story or poem
representing your relationship with your siblings.
(or being an only child)

"Make your mistakes, take your chances, look silly, but keep on going. Don't freeze up."

Thomas Wolfe, *You Can't Go Home Again*

A drawing, short story or poem representing a flaw you actually like.

Date: ___ / ___ / _____

"What kind of life can you have in a house without books?"

Sherman Alexie, *Flight*

What are your three favorite books and why?

Date: ___ / ___ / _____

**"Time is the coin of your life. You spend it.
Do not allow others to spend it for you."**

Carl Sandburg

A drawing, short story or poem
representing the people who've used you.
(And how you claimed your independence.)

Date: ___ / ___ / _____

"All you need is love.
But a little chocolate now and then doesn't hurt."

Charles M. Schulz

What five people are triggering you the most? Why?

Date: ___ / ___ / _____

"The pleasure of all reading is doubled when one lives with another who shares the same books."

Katherine Mansfield

A drawing, short story or poem
representing your deepest feelings when it comes to love.

"Numbing the pain for a while will make it worse when you finally feel it."

J.K. Rowling, *Harry Potter*

Your favorite ways to sabotage your own happiness.

Date: ___ / ___ / _____

"In a time of destruction,
create something."

Maxine Hong Kingston

A drawing, short story or poem about the last time you hit rock bottom. (Give it a touch of hope, honoring how you were able to pull yourself through!)

"When the whole world is silent, even one voice becomes powerful."

Malala Yousafzai, *I Am Malala*

If doing your best was good enough,
what would that do to your feeling of happiness?

_____

_____

_____

_____

_____

_____

_____

_____

_____

_____

_____

_____

_____

_____

_____

_____

_____

_____

_____

_____

_____

_____

_____

_____

_____

_____

_____

_____

_____

Date: ___ / ___ / _____

"So many things become beautiful
when you really look."

Lauren Oliver, *Before I Fall*

A drawing, short story or poem
portraying something small, almost insignificant, that is beautiful.

**"I don't know that love changes.
People change. Circumstances change."**

Nicholas Sparks

A drawing, short story or poem
about what you are trying to avoid in a relationship.

**"Worry never robs tomorrow of its sorrow,
but only saps today of its strength."**

A.J. Cronin

The maximum you think you could handle and deserve
when it comes to your health and physical appearance.

"Have no fear of perfection - you'll never reach it."

Salvador Dali

The maximum you think you could handle and deserve when it comes to your social life.

_____
_____
_____
_____
_____
_____
_____
_____
_____
_____
_____
_____
_____
_____
_____
_____
_____
_____
_____
_____
_____
_____
_____
_____
_____
_____

"Children must be taught how to think, not what to think."

Margaret Mead

How your emotional intelligence could serve you in your career.

_____

_____

_____

_____

_____

_____

_____

_____

_____

_____

_____

_____

_____

_____

_____

_____

_____

_____

_____

_____

_____

_____

_____

_____

_____

_____

_____

_____

Date: ___ / ___ / _____

"When people don't express themselves, they die one piece at a time."

Laurie Halse Anderson, *Speak*

What are you waiting for?

_____
_____
_____
_____
_____
_____
_____
_____
_____
_____
_____
_____
_____
_____
_____
_____
_____
_____
_____
_____
_____
_____
_____
_____
_____
_____

Date: ___ / ___ / _____

"Lighthouses don't go running all over an island looking for boats to save; they just stand there shining."

Anne Lamott

Who do you secretly wait for and why?

_____
_____
_____
_____
_____
_____
_____
_____
_____
_____
_____
_____
_____
_____
_____
_____
_____
_____
_____
_____
_____
_____
_____
_____
_____
_____
_____
_____

Date: ___ / ___ / _____

"You only get one life
It's actually your duty to live it as fully as possible."

Jojo Moyes, Me Before You

Three statements you wanna live by.

_____
_____
_____
_____
_____
_____
_____
_____
_____
_____
_____
_____
_____
_____
_____
_____
_____
_____
_____
_____
_____
_____
_____
_____
_____
_____
_____
_____

Date: ___ / ___ / _____

"Beauty is only skin deep,
but ugly goes clean to the bone."

Dorothy Parker

Where in your life could you use more integrity?
How can you make this happen?

_____
_____
_____
_____
_____
_____
_____
_____
_____
_____
_____
_____
_____
_____
_____
_____
_____
_____
_____
_____
_____
_____
_____
_____
_____
_____
_____

Date: ___ / ___ / _____

"If you do not tell the truth about yourself you cannot tell it about other people."

Virginia Woolf

What kind of recklessness do you secretly like?

"If I'd observed all the rules
I'd never have got anywhere."

Marilyn Monroe

What rules are standing in the way of your happiness right now?

_____

_____

_____

_____

_____

_____

_____

_____

_____

_____

_____

_____

_____

_____

_____

_____

_____

_____

_____

_____

_____

_____

_____

_____

_____

_____

_____

_____

_____

Date: ___ / ___ / _____

"I wasn't actually in love, but I felt a sort of tender curiosity."

F. Scott Fitzgerald, The Great Gatsby

What kind of persons make you curious?

"I'm tough, I'm ambitious, and I know exactly what I want. If that makes me a bitch, okay."

Madonna

Your thought on ambition.

_____
_____
_____
_____
_____
_____
_____
_____
_____
_____
_____
_____
_____
_____
_____
_____
_____
_____
_____
_____
_____
_____
_____
_____
_____
_____
_____
_____
_____

Date: ___ / ___ / _____

"That it will never come again
is what makes life so sweet."

Emily Dickinson

A drawing, poem or short story
about your best sexual experience or a sexual fantasy.

Date: ___ / ___ / _____

"As if you were on fire from within.
The moon lives in the lining of your skin."

Pablo Neruda

A drawing, poem or short story about your definition of sex appeal.

"You know what charm is: a way of getting the answer yes without having asked any clear question."

Albert Camus, The Fall

A drawing, poem or short story about seduction.

**"Don't be afraid of death; be afraid of an unlived life.
You don't have to live forever, you just have to live."**

Natalie Babbitt, *Tuck Everlasting*

A drawing, poem or short story about living life to the fullest.

"It's a lot easier to be lost than found. It's the reason we're always searching and rarely discovered--so many locks not enough keys."

Sarah Dessen, *Lock and Key*

A drawing, poem or short story about your journey of self-discovery.

Date: ___ / ___ / _____

"How did it get so late so soon?"

Dr. Seuss

A drawing, poem or short story about women being together.

"Atticus told me to delete the adjectives and I'd have the facts."

Harper Lee, *To Kill a Mockingbird*

A drawing, poem or short story about being strong.

"Don't let mental blocks control you. Set yourself free. Confront your fear and turn the mental blocks into building blocks."

Dr. Roopleen

What kind of person always makes you feel jealous?
What has been the influence of being jealous in your life?

_____
_____
_____
_____
_____
_____
_____
_____
_____
_____
_____
_____
_____
_____
_____
_____
_____
_____
_____
_____
_____
_____
_____
_____
_____
_____
_____
_____
_____

Date: ___ / ___ / _____

"Everyone you will ever meet knows something you don't."

Bill Nye

A drawing, poem or short story about wisdom.

Date: ___ / ___ / _____

"You will do foolish things,
but do them with enthusiasm."

Colette

How could you loosen up a bit more?

_____

_____

_____

_____

_____

_____

_____

_____

_____

_____

_____

_____

_____

_____

_____

_____

_____

_____

_____

_____

_____

_____

_____

_____

_____

_____

_____

Date: ___ / ___ / _____

"All I ever wanted was to reach out and touch another human being not just with my hands but with my heart."

Tahereh Mafi, *Shatter Me*

Three good deeds you could do this week.

_____
_____
_____
_____
_____
_____
_____
_____
_____
_____
_____
_____
_____
_____
_____
_____
_____
_____
_____
_____
_____
_____
_____
_____
_____
_____
_____

Date: ___ / ___ / _____

"Today a reader, tomorrow a leader."

Margaret Fuller

Pick an old photo of yourself that is at least three years old.
Take a good look at the photo, and then reflect on it.

_____
_____
_____
_____
_____
_____
_____
_____
_____
_____
_____
_____
_____
_____
_____
_____
_____
_____
_____
_____
_____
_____
_____
_____
_____
_____
_____
_____
_____

"Romance is the glamour which turns the dust of everyday life into a golden haze. "

Elinor Glyn

Write down your bucket list.
Which item could you actually do this year?

Date: ___ / ___ / _____

**"Question everything. Your love, your religion, your passion.
If you don't have questions, you'll never find answers."**

Colleen Hoover, Slammed

What do you need to question?
Why?

_____
_____
_____
_____
_____
_____
_____
_____
_____
_____
_____
_____
_____
_____
_____
_____
_____
_____
_____
_____
_____
_____
_____
_____
_____
_____
_____

"Every life has death and every light has shadow. Be content to stand in the light and let the shadow fall where it will."

Mary Stewart, *The Hollow Hills*

What frustrates you the most in a romantic relationship?

**"You cannot pick and choose
what parts of her to love."**

Sarah J. Maas, *Heir of Fire*

What frustrates you the most about your sex life?

_____
_____
_____
_____
_____
_____
_____
_____
_____
_____
_____
_____
_____
_____
_____
_____
_____
_____
_____
_____
_____
_____
_____
_____
_____
_____
_____

Date: ___ / ___ / _____

**"Never attempt to teach a pig to sing;
it wastes your time and annoys the pig."**

Robert Heinlein, *Time Enough for Love*

How could you help yourself this week?

**"To lose balance sometimes for love
is part of living a balanced life."**

Elizabeth Gilbert, *Eat, Pray, Love*

A drawing, short story or poem about living a balanced life.

"Whoever is careless with the truth in small matters cannot be trusted with important matters."

Albert Einstein

A drawing, short story or poem about integrity.

"The longer I live, the more I observe that carrying around anger is the most debilitating to the person who bears it."

Katharine Graham

A drawing, short story or poem about forgiving someone who'd hurt you in the past.

"I myself have never been able to find out precisely what feminism is: I only know that people call me a feminist whenever I express sentiments that differentiate me from a doormat."

Rebecca West

A drawing, short story or poem to celebrate self-expression.

Date: ___ / ___ / _____

"My course is set for an uncharted sea."

Dante Alighieri

Your ideal three weeks of traveling.

_____
_____
_____
_____
_____
_____
_____
_____
_____
_____
_____
_____
_____
_____
_____
_____
_____
_____
_____
_____
_____
_____
_____
_____
_____
_____
_____
_____

"I guess that's just part of loving people: You have to give things up. Sometimes you even have to give them up."

Lauren Oliver, *Delirium*

What do you have to give up to live a more authentic life?

"Through my education, I didn't just develop skills, I didn't just develop the ability to learn, but I developed confidence."

Michelle Obama

Is your social life a true reflection of who you actually are? Why or why not?

Date: ___ / ___ / _____

"Courage is found in unlikely places."

J.R.R. Tolkien

A drawing, short story, poem, roadmap or anything...
to express your life vision.

"Every time you are tempted to react in the same old way, ask if you want to be a prisoner of the past or a pioneer of the future."

Deepak Chopra

What in the past still has a grip on you in a negative way?
What could you do to loosen its grip?

"The only real prison is fear, and the only real freedom is freedom from fear."

Aung San Suu Kyi

Your personal manifesto on how to live life.
(see also the next page;)!

"Remember, remember, this is now, and now, and now.
Live it, feel it, cling to it.
I want to become acutely aware of all I've taken for granted."

Sylvia Plath

Take your personal manifesto, and try to make art out of it.
Just give it your best shot, it's up to you how:)

"There is something delicious about writing the first words of a story. You never quite know where they'll take you."

Beatrix Potter

Where are the choices you've made in your love life, most likely going to take you? Is the answer satisfying?

If not, how could you change course...

Date: ___ / ___ / _____

"May the odds be ever in your favor!"

Suzanne Collins, *The Hunger Games*

A drawing, short story or poem about luck.

Date: ___ / ___ / _____

"Scared is what you're feeling.
Brave is what you're doing."

Emma Donoghue, *Room*

A drawing, short story or poem that portrays your image.

Date: ___ / ___ / _____

**"I wrote the story myself.
It's about a girl who lost her reputation and never missed it."**

Mae West

A drawing, short story or poem that portrays your authentic self.

"She had always wanted words, she loved them; grew up on them. Words gave her clarity, brought reason, shape."

Michael Ondaatje, *The English Patient*

A drawing, short story or poem about what words can't express.

**"Great Minds Discuss Ideas.
Average Minds Discuss Events.
Small Minds Discuss People."**

Eleanor Roosevelt

What ideas would you like to discuss?
Can you do this with the people closest to you?

_____
_____
_____
_____
_____
_____
_____
_____
_____
_____
_____
_____
_____
_____
_____
_____
_____
_____
_____
_____
_____
_____
_____
_____
_____
_____
_____
_____

Date: ___ / ___ / _____

"When someone is cruel or acts like a bully, you don't stoop to their level. No, our motto is, when they go low, we go high."

Michelle Obama

The last time you spoke up for something greater than yourself.

202

"If you don't know, the thing to do is not to get scared, but to learn."

Ayn Rand, *Atlas Shrugged*

What events are often triggering your negative self-dialogue?

Date: ___ / ___ / _____

"The most common way people give up their power is by thinking they don't have any."

Alice Walker

How would you like people to remember you?

_____
_____
_____
_____
_____
_____
_____
_____
_____
_____
_____
_____
_____
_____
_____
_____
_____
_____
_____
_____
_____
_____
_____
_____
_____
_____

Date: ___ / ___ / _____

"Maybe ever'body in the whole damn world is scared of each other."

John Steinbeck, *Of Mice and Men*

What was your favorite age growing up?

_____
_____
_____
_____
_____
_____
_____
_____
_____
_____
_____
_____
_____
_____
_____
_____
_____
_____
_____
_____
_____
_____
_____
_____
_____
_____
_____
_____

Date: ___ / ___ / _____

"Instead of looking at the past, I put myself ahead twenty years
and try to look at what I need to do now in order to get there then"

Diana Ross

A drawing, poem or short story
portraying your hopes for the future.

Date: ___ / ___ / _____

"Live in the sunshine, swim the sea, drink the wild air."

Ralph Waldo Emerson

How does your ideal morning look like?
And your ideal night?

_____
_____
_____
_____
_____
_____
_____
_____
_____
_____
_____
_____
_____
_____
_____
_____
_____
_____
_____
_____
_____
_____
_____
_____
_____
_____

Date: ___ / ___ / _____

"A Woman in harmony with her spirit is like a river flowing. She goes where she will without pretense and arrives at her destination prepared to be herself and only herself."

Maya Angelou

When was the last time you felt truly alive?

_____
_____
_____
_____
_____
_____
_____
_____
_____
_____
_____
_____
_____
_____
_____
_____
_____
_____
_____
_____
_____
_____
_____
_____
_____
_____

Date: ___ / ___ / _____

"The best things in life make you sweaty."

Edgar Allan Poe

What is the benefit of being patient?
How could you improve your own art of being patience?

_____
_____
_____
_____
_____
_____
_____
_____
_____
_____
_____
_____
_____
_____
_____
_____
_____
_____
_____
_____
_____
_____
_____
_____
_____
_____

"You know, when it works, love is pretty amazing. It's not overrated. There's a reason for all those songs."

Sarah Dessen, *This Lullaby*

What would be a completely different approach to improve your dating/love life?

"To define is to limit."

Oscar Wilde, *The Picture of Dorian Gray*

How much personal time do you actually need every day, to function best?

_____
_____
_____
_____
_____
_____
_____
_____
_____
_____
_____
_____
_____
_____
_____
_____
_____
_____
_____
_____
_____
_____
_____
_____
_____
_____

"Things we lose have a way of coming back to us in the end, if not always in the way we expect."

JK Rowling, *Harry Potter and the Order of the Phoenix*

What three things could you do to make this month great?

"No need to hurry. No need to sparkle. No need to be anybody but oneself."

Virginia Woolf, *A Room of One's Own / Three Guineas*

Write a letter to yourself, to be opened one year from now.

Courage, Love & Happiness

A Self-Discovery Journal For Women

Follow us on Instagram

For promotions, giveaways and newest arrivals

Instagram: 21exercises_journals

Made in United States
Orlando, FL
14 December 2021

11675531R00136